Crested Gecko Made Simple:

Detailed Guide on How to Effectively Raise Crested Gecko as Pets & Other Purposes; Includes Its Care& Diseases; Feeding; Choosing a Breed; Its Home & So On

By

Markus J. Muench

Copyright@2020

TABLE OF CONTENTS

CHAPTER ONE

INTRODUCTION

Crested geckos as they are called were once thought to be wiped out, however were rediscovered around 1994. From that point forward, their notoriety as pets has persistently expanded. They are a low-upkeep pet, appropriate for youngsters or fledgling reptile proprietors who have brief period to give to their every day care. One of their particular highlights is their eyelashes, which is the reason they are at times called eyelash geckos. These reptiles hail from New Caledonia, an island nation off the bank of Australia.

-Normal name: Crested gecko, New Caledonian peaked gecko, eyelash gecko

-Logical name: Rhacodactylus ciliates

-Grown-up size: 7 to 9 inches, including their prehensile tails

-Future: 10 to 20 years

CHAPTER TWO

CRESTED GECKO BEHAVIOR PLUS TEMPERAMENT AS WELL AS HOW TO HOUSE THEM

Peaked geckos arrive in a wide cluster of hues and markings (transforms). They get their name from the bordered peak that starts over their eyes and runs down their necks and backs; however the size of the peak differs.

Peaked geckos have particular toe cushions that permit them to move along vertical surfaces easily, and their prehensile tails add to their agility. They are likewise phenomenal jumpers.

Peaked geckos as a rule have generally compliant demeanors, however they are somewhat sketchy, and care is required when dealing with them. They don't typically like dealing with, so dodge it if conceivable. They may attempt to hop away from you, which can harm them. Peaked geckos may drop their tails whenever being taken care of generally or they endeavor to move away; in contrast to different geckos, they won't recover their tails.

They will possibly chomp on the off chance that they feel undermined. Nibbles are alarming however they don't do any harm and are not sufficiently able to cause dying.

Lodging the Crested Gecko

At least a 20-gallon tall terrarium is adequate for a grown-up, yet a bigger tank is better. Crested or peaked geckos are arboreal, dynamic, as well as need heaps of vertical space for climbing, so a tall tank is liked. A few peaked geckos can be housed in a tall 29-gallon terrarium. Guys are regional, so keep just a single male for each tank. You can utilize a glass terrarium with a screened side for ventilation, however a few managers incline toward screened walled in areas.

Crested geckos demand space to climb, so give a blend of branches, driftwood, plug bark, bamboo, and plants at an assortment of statures and directions. Every day, you should eliminate all uneaten food and spot and clean to eliminate defecation. Clean the whole terrarium and its designs at any rate once a month utilizing reptile-safe disinfectants. Contingent upon the substrate, you should supplant it week after week or month to month to forestall bacterial development.

Warmth

As heartless animals, everything reptiles require to control their internal heat level. A daytime temperature slope of 72 F to 80 F, or 22 C to 26.5 C, ought to be given for peaked geckos a drop around evening time to 65 F to 75 F, or 18 C to 24 C. Screen with temperatures measures to guarantee the pen doesn't overheat. Peaked geckos get worried at higher temperatures. A low-wattage red evening time bulb makes a decent warmth source and it additionally permits you to see the reptile around evening time when it is generally dynamic. Try not to rest a **warmth source on the head of the tank as these climbing geckos could get excessively close and get scorched.**

Why Heat plus Light Are So Important for Your Pet Reptile

Light

Crested or peaked geckos are nighttime; actually, they needn't bother with uncommon UVB lighting. In any case, a few specialists propose a low degree of UVB lighting, say around 5 percent, is helpful for generally speaking reptile wellbeing. Any additional lighting will bring the temperature up in the walled in area, so screen that. Additionally, give a gecko hideaway so geckos can move away from the light on the off chance that they need.

Dampness

Peaked geckos need a moderate to high dampness level. Focus on 60 percent during the day and 80 percent at night. Get a hygrometer (mugginess measure) to screen levels every day. Give dampness standard clouding with warm, sifted water. Contingent upon your confine arrangement, you may need to fog it a couple of times each day to keep the stickiness up. Continuously ensure the pen is very much clouded around evening time when the geckos are generally dynamic. On the off chance that you are not around during the day or can't genuinely fog the nook, get a programmed mister or fogger to add mugginess to the enclosure at coordinated stretches.

Substrate

Most pet proprietors utilize a substrate to line the base of the enclosure. While choosing a substrate for a gecko, think about pet wellbeing, simplicity of cleaning, and if the substrate helps in holding dampness. Ideal substrates for a peaked gecko are coconut fiber bedding, greenery, or peat. You can likewise utilize paper or paper towels, in spite of the fact that these are not as alluring.

Peaked geckos are fairly inclined to ingesting substrate while chasing; if so for yours, utilization sphagnum greenery (either alone or over another substrate likes coconut fiber) or paper towels. Paper towels are suggested for adolescents as they are bound to swallow different substrates coincidentally.

Albeit alluring, rock or stones are not an appropriate substrate since it is hard to clean altogether and normally. Stay away from reptile sand and non-natural soil substrate, since these are gulping perils.

CHAPTER THREE

CRESTED GECKO MEALS AS WELL AS HEALTH CHALLENGES YOU SHOULD KNOW

Food and Water

Since they are nighttime, feed peaked geckos at night. Feed adolescents every day and grown-ups three times each week.

A business peaked gecko diet is typically all around acknowledged amount and is the most effortless approach to guarantee an even, nutritious eating routine. Supplement that food with crickets and other prey bugs (insects, wax worms, silkworms). Abstain from taking care of mealworms, since they have a hard, indigestible exoskeleton. For assortment and to permit the gecko to practice his chasing senses, feed as much prey creepy crawlies at once as the gecko enthusiastically eats.

To support your reptile's nutrient and mineral admission, dust the bugs with a calcium/nutrient D3 powdered enhancement three times each week. Residue prey things with a multivitamin powder supplement once every week.

Crested geckos do eat organic produce a few times each week. Attempt crushed natural product or jostled infant food. Top choices incorporate bananas, peaches, nectarines, apricots, papaya, mangoes, pears, and enthusiasm natural product.

On the off chance that you experience issues finding a business gecko diet, give a mix of bug prey things and natural product. This choice isn't the most adjusted eating regimen, however it will do the trick when absolutely necessary or for a brief period. For this situation, your best creepy crawly decision is crickets with a periodic expansion of different bugs for assortment.

Furnish a little shallow water dish with new water day by day; however they will probably want to drink water beads from leaves in the damp natural surroundings.

Normal Health Problems

Geckos are inclined to a couple of medical issues that are treatable by an exotics veterinarian.

Mouth decay or stomatitis: Signs incorporate overabundance bodily fluid and redness around the mouth.

Respiratory contamination: Symptoms are wheezing or slobbering.

Skin issues: A rash, indicative of a parasitic contamination; lopsided or trouble shedding which might be brought about by lacking nook dampness

To forestall any wounds and wounds, check out the confine and roll out any important improvements if necessary. Shroud any wires, ensure lights can't be reached, separate confine mates if there is any harassing, document any sharp edges on the adornments and wood branches, secure frill and so on.

Wounds and indentations ought to recuperate well, yet make a point to keep the confine clean to forestall any contamination.

You can even move your peaked gecko to a Kritter Keeper or other terrarium for now if there are any open injuries. Apply a smidgen of anti-toxin treatment on open injuries to forestall contaminations.

Eye issues and contaminations in peaked geckos

Crested or peaked gecko tainted eyes - growing and liquid development

Peaked geckos may create eye contaminations, and tainted eyes ought to generally look swollen and greater because of liquid development. In the event that there is any release and growing, at that point it's most likely an eye contamination.

However, in the event that there is no expanding or release, at that point it's most likely an inward eye harm or waterfall. In the event that you presume a contamination, utilize antimicrobial eye drops to treat diseases. In the event that it doesn't pass or in the event that you speculate a waterfall, take your peaked gecko to the vet.

Lack of hydration and spewing forth in a peaked gecko

Your crested or peaked gecko may get dried out in the event that it doesn't drink enough water. Some peaked geckos experience difficulty drinking water from a dish, particularly if your gecko is youthful or if the dish it excessively profound.

In addition, on the off chance that you feed your peaked gecko with just dry nourishments, it may get dried out. Complete powder diet must be blended in with water and if offering bugs – have a water bowl consistently. Any disorder and parasites may likewise cause lack of hydration.

On the off chance that you can see that your peaked gecko can't drink water from a bowl, or if your gecko is debilitated, apply water drops on its nose and it will lick them. Fog the enclosure once every day for grown-ups and two times per day for infants and adolescents. Keep the enclosure mugginess ideal (60-70%), and have a computerized dampness measure to check the levels.

Your peaked gecko may experience the ill effects of disgorging in the event that you handle your peaked gecko straight subsequent to taking care of or if temperatures in the tank are excessively low.

These components can forestall processing, so don't pressure your gecko subsequent to taking care of. Inward parasites can likewise cause disgorging and spewing. In the event that indications don't go in the wake of checking temperatures and lessening taking care of and distressing circumstances, take your gecko crap for a fecal test.

To set up gecko's crap for a stool test, gather it in a little pack with a zipper and refrigerate it. Try not to freeze the crap.

Inside parasites in peaked geckos

Coccidiosis in peaked geckos is an inside parasite

Coccidia

There are various kinds of parasites that can influence your peaked or crested gecko. A few parasites are ordinary and live in the gut greenery, so stool test is important to screen their levels if your gecko is wiped out.

Numerous worms are additionally typical in peaked or crested gecko's stomach related framework, so tests are important to check whether their levels in the dung are excessively high. Parasites that can influence your peaked gecko are following:

Protozoa –, say Coccidia, Cryptosporidium,
Flagellates

Worms – roundworms, Nematodes
(pinworms)

Entamoeba

All inside parasites in extraordinary numbers
will cause loss of craving, dormancy,
looseness of the bowels, weight reduction
and drying out. Take a feces test, refrigerate
it (don't freeze) and take it to the vet for
assessment.

Steam cleaner for a reptile vivarium

Steam Cleaners Sanitizing Strength Plus Surfaces It Can Handle

You should clean the tank and purify all the assistants to forestall reinfection. An awesome method to clean peaked gecko's tank is by utilizing a steam cleaner that makes use of warmed constrained steam that is warmed to around 200 degrees F.

Cryptosporidiosis is one of the most exceedingly awful reptile diseases and as a rule causes passing if untreated (because of weight reduction, stomach related problems and ailing health). It frequently contaminates panther geckos, instead of peaked geckos, however. They can be seen under the magnifying instrument and treated right away with parasitic medications.

On the off chance that you notice any worms in the crap, isolate your peaked gecko straight away – move it to a basic holder with paper towels.

Coccidiosis spreads very quickly, and you should be mindful so as to forestall reinfection. Sterilizing the tank and adornments as well as moving your gecko to a littler holder will be the best way to forestall reinfection while gecko is accepting treatment.

Salmonella are microorganisms that live in the gut of peaked geckos, and different reptiles. They are a piece of ordinary gut greenery, and don't bring on any issues in peaked or crested geckos.

Proprietors may contract Salmonella, so washing hands subsequent to taking care of peaked geckos or cleaning the tank is significant. Try not to eat when contacting your gecko and don't wash extras in the kitchen sink. Salmonellosis causes fever, loose bowels, issues and fever in individuals.

Outside parasites in peaked geckos

Peaked or crested geckos may get tainted with bugs, however this doesn't occur frequently. Bugs can be difficult to eliminate and it will require some investment to clear the invasion. Red parasites can be seen on peaked geckos, however this is very uncommon. To eliminate parasites, you should utilize vermin splash, or use cotton buds plunged in oil or liquor and eliminate them physically.

CHAPTER FOUR

PICKING YOUR CRESTED GECKO PLUS THE VARIOUS TYPES YOU SHOULD KNOW

Peaked geckos are generally sold, basically on the grounds that they are so natural to think about and have such bright airs contrasted with different reptiles. Despite the fact that they're broadly accessible at pet stores, attempt to get your peaked or crested gecko from a trustworthy reproducer. You can hope to pay $40 to $150 for a peaked gecko—the cost increments with the uncommonness of the shading or transform.

When choosing your gecko, ensure your gecko can climb well, has a straight spine, and no noticeable ribs or pelvic bones.

It ought to show up enthusiastic and alert. Likewise, it ought to have brilliant eyes, just as a spotless nose and vent or fecal opening.

Normal pet gecko types for novices

-Various Species of Geckos:

-White-Lined Gecko Species

-Panther Gecko Species

Tokay Gecko Species.

CHAPTER FIVE

THE PROS AS WELL AS CONS OF CRESTED GECKO YOU SHOULD BE AWARE OF

Is it accurate to say that you are contemplating turning into a glad proprietor of a delightful peaked gecko or few? Be that as it may, is peaked or crested gecko a decent pet? Let's find out!

Crested or Peaked gecko as a pet – The vital pros

1. Little tank size

Peaked geckos are little and needn't bother with much space – a little 15-20 gallon tank for a solitary grown-up peaked gecko is adequate. For instance, a 18x18x24 Exo Terra tank (around 33 gallons) would be appropriate for 2 peaked geckos.

For as long as a year old (around 10-15 grams) you can keep your peaked or crested gecko in a littler 6-10 gallon Kritter Keeper or a little terrarium.

By and large, 20 gallons for every each peaked geckos will give loads of room, and 10 gallons is the absolute minimum Kindly note that peaked geckos require vertical confines for climbing.

2. Grown-up peaked or crested geckos can live respectively

While you ought not to keep hatchling, infant or adolescent peaked geckos together, you can keep grown-ups together effectively. This is on the grounds that littler peaked geckos will cause each other pressure and will go after food and space.

When peaked geckos arrive at 20 grams, can be between 1-2 years of age, they can commonly live respectively.

Notwithstanding, you should not house guys together. The best proportion is 1 male and 1-2 females or scarcely any females together.

Indeed, try to watch females and male peaked geckos during the rearing season. In the event that a male makes pressure on a female, you should isolate them.

3. Most peaked geckos are agreeable

How Friendly Are Crested Geckos?

The initial 1-3 weeks after you bring your new peaked gecko home will be unpleasant for the gecko. You should generally disregard it and to allow it to adapt. This is ordinary with most reptiles, however.

After your peaked gecko becomes accustomed to its new home and you begin taking care of it normally, it will get lenient toward dealing with. More youthful peaked geckos are very unpredictable and nervous, however with age, they calm down additional. Particularly in the event that you handle your peaked gecko routinely, at any rate not many times each week.

4. Peaked geckos don't need confounded arrangements

Peaked geckos don't need particular reptile UVB lighting, if any whatsoever.

Additionally, you shouldn't have to warm the peaked gecko's tank if the room temperature is ideal!

Peaked geckos approve of normal light. Roughly 75 degrees in the warm side and 68-70 F in the cool side are extremely ideal for a peaked gecko. You can at present have low UVB (5.0) lighting in your peaked gecko's tank for extra D3 creation.

On the off chance that you have to light the tank, you may utilize a major scope of bulbs – regular sunshine, full-range or glaring lights are altogether reasonable.

5. Basic eating regimen

A great many people, particularly those new to reptiles, will in general pick peaked geckos in light of the fact that they have basic weight control plans. The thing is, peaked or crested geckos can be taken care of just with a peaked gecko diet (CGD), which is healthfully adjusted and reasonable for your peaked gecko. This is a food in a powder structure, which is blended in with water and offered to your peaked gecko.

While it is useful to offer feeder bugs to your peaked gecko a few times per week, it's not required on the off chance that you can't have bugs in your home.

There are even peaked gecko eats less carbs that have squashed bugs added to them.

Not many of the most respectable brands for peaked gecko food are Pangea and Repashy. Obviously there are different brands, as well. So taking care of your peaked gecko just with CGD is conceivable.

6. Lovely looks

Are Crested Geckos Good Pets?

Peaked geckos are simply lovely! They look like little mythical serpents from fantasies as well as books. Peaked geckos have dazzling eyes with little lashes, excellent feet with clingy cushions, smooth skin and a long tail!

Regardless of whether a peaked gecko drops its tail, it would not meddle with its way of life at all, yet it won't develop back.

7. Loads of different transforms accessible

This merit is a different point. There are so numerous wonderful peaked gecko transforms that will make you need an ever increasing number of peaked geckos!

Most peaked gecko proprietors start with one peaked gecko and afterward get more, not in any event, contingent upon a transform. Peaked geckos are simply too adorable to even consider stopping at one.

You can discover a post about peaked gecko transforms here.

8. Great accessibility

Peaked geckos are generally accessible as pets for buy or reception. It isn't elusive a peaked gecko that you might want. Transforms may cost more, however when all is said in done, peaked geckos are not costly to purchase and allowed to receive.

9. Long-living and very strong

Crested or peaked geckos have a life expectancy of around 10-20 years in bondage. In the event that you give appropriate consideration, your peaked gecko will live for 15 and even as long as 20 years.

Peaked geckos are likewise very solid and don't frequently experience the ill effects of an excessive number of issues whenever kept accurately. On the off chance that you want to keep a peaked gecko, kindly give a great deal of consideration to confine stickiness, not very high or low, ensure warming and lighting is adequate and so forth.

In the case of taking care of live bugs, try to gut-load them for 1 day before offering. Additionally dust with supplements. Calcium, nutrient D3 and other mineral and nutrient lack can gradually execute your peaked geckos.

Find out about peaked gecko's eating regimen – remembering nourishments and enhancements for this post.

10. Simple to raise

Peaked geckos are very simple to raise. They begin demonstrating rearing enthusiasm at the age of 18 two years, contingent upon development rate.

Crested or peaked gecko drawbacks cons

1. Peaked geckos are little

Is Crested Gecko a Good Or Nice Pet

In the event that you might want a reptile that has an enormous strong body, at that point a peaked gecko isn't one of them. Peaked geckos are tiny and may be trying to hold appropriately without worrying to pound it. Grown-up peaked geckos regularly arrive at 30-55 grams.

This particularly applies to infant peaked geckos. You ought to abstain from dealing with a peaked gecko less than 10 grams to an extreme (up to 10 a year old). Peaked geckos are additionally jittery, particularly youthful ones.

You should be either certain or handle your peaked gecko when plunking down or in a sheltered zone to keep escapes and tumbles from statures.

2. Peaked geckos are crepuscular

On the off chance that you might want a pet reptile that is dynamic during the **day, at that point a peaked gecko isn't one of them. Peaked geckos are** crepuscular – which implies that they become dynamic towards the late night.

In any case, uplifting news is, peaked geckos are not boisterous around evening time. They can peep and make scarcely any clamors while moving around; however that ought not to be an issue.

3. Some peaked geckos can get forceful

Most peaked geckos are mild and benevolent, however now and then, they can unexpectedly get forceful. While forceful peaked geckos nibbles and open mouth expanding will be more for startling and not liable to draw blood, it can in any case become an issue. It may influence taking care of them and your peaked gecko's overall prosperity.

There are various reasons why a peaked gecko may turn furious, for instance reproducing period, arrangement change and that's only the tip of the iceberg. While more often than not it passes, some peaked geckos remain forceful for quite a long time on.

4. Peaked geckos are delicate to warm and different components

Peaked geckos require warm conditions to live in, and a temperature angle from warm to cool is obligatory. In the event that there is no temperature angle in the tank, peaked gecko can rapidly overheat and pass on!

Same goes to moistness – ensure it's not in every case high during the day, you should let the tank dry for scarcely any prior hours moistening once more. Peaked geckos require moistening 1-2 times each day.

Mugginess ought to be around 65-75% during the day, with a morning period dropping to half and ascending to 85-90% soon after moistening. Give the heaviest clouding towards the night.

Changing of the tank, area, adornments and more can likewise make your peaked gecko pushed. Be that as it may, most pet reptiles respond to any changes. Ensure they are not all unexpected.

5. Peaked gecko can undoubtedly drop its tail

Peaked geckos can get effectively frightened on the off chance that you make any abrupt moves. This can bring about a tail drop. There are numerous reasons why peaked geckos can drop their tail. At times a peaked gecko can even drop its tail without a legitimate explanation.

Be that as it may, don't stress – a peaked gecko without a tail can carry on with a long glad life and it won't influence anything. For the initial hardly any days, your peaked gecko will become acclimated to climbing and holding without a tail, yet that is about it. Most peaked geckos in the wild live without a tail, and it's ordinary.

CHAPTER SIX

MORE ON THE HEALTH/WELL-BEING OF CRESTED GECKO AS WELL AS OTHER FACTS FOR YOU

Wellbeing

Keeping up peaked gecko wellbeing is simple when you start with a sound creature.

Purchase from raisers that have a decent notoriety. In the event that you get an opportunity to see the gecko face to face, you can assess outer signs that demonstrate great wellbeing. To pick a sound pet, search for the indications of a solid gecko:

Alert: despite the fact that peaked geckos are nighttime, they ought to respond to you getting them and analyzing them. Some are more laid back, and once woken up, will essentially gaze at you with an inquisitive look. A debilitated creature may shake and feel unequal in your grasp.

Clean: Healthy peaked geckos are not infrequently influenced by skin parasites, nor do they have release around their nose, eyes or vent (where they discharge). Numerous geckos have raised, hued scales or Dalmatian spots that ought not be confused with parasites, wounds or injuries. An "unfired" gecko may seem powder-colored, yet this is on the grounds that their shading is constrained by their disposition and season of day or night. Geckos in shed may have some adhered to their heads, body or appendages; shed adhered to the toes ought to be taken out as this can cause the loss of digits.

Stocky: Compared to different geckos, peaked geckos are positively fabricated. Hip bones around the pelvis ought not jut. Notwithstanding, ribs can be seen usually in youthful creatures and in grown-ups relying upon the point you see them. Grown-up creatures will in general be plumper around the throat and chest. A dainty appearance could show parchedness as opposed to helpless eating or malady.

Keeping up a Healthy Gecko

Appropriate eating routine and cultivation is basic to the wellbeing all things considered, and it is imperative to ensure your peaked gecko gets the most ideal consideration.

Stress

Limiting pressure is additionally critical to keeping up your peaked gecko's wellbeing. With a well arrangement walled in area, you limit everyday worry by giving your peaked gecko a protected home with a lot of spots to stow away. Stress can carry inactive issues to the surface; a subdued invulnerable framework from stress can initiate a flare-up of parasites that were typically kept in line. Focused on creatures that don't eat well, which can bring about nourishing issues.

Lack of hydration

Peaked geckos can undoubtedly experience the ill effects of parchedness, which can prompt passing in a shockingly brief timeframe. Give a water bowl or potentially utilize a splash container to fog the walled in areas on a daily premise. Open screen tanks or 20 gallon tanks turned on end offer a lot of ventilation however don't hold dampness well. Wrapping with plastic or utilizing plexi-glass boards to cover half of the screen can help in holding dampness. A lay box or moist stow away can be a useful retreat. A little Tupperware or glad ware holder loaded up with sodden natural soil, coco fiber, peat greenery or even paper towels can offer your gecko a chance to self-manage dampness levels. Be that as it may, screen for shape development as they may follow in food or utilize their retreats as a latrine!

On the off chance that you have your geckos in a plastic tub, make certain there is satisfactory ventilation. A lot of dampness can develop and cause respiratory issues and additionally form development inside the walled in area. We select water bowls joined with light showering.

Isolate

Continuously be certain that fresh debuts don't come into contact with your set up pets!

A multi day least QT period is suggested. 30-60 days is commonly standard from quality raisers. A multi day isolate is suggested for geckos originating from obscure sources or a pet store condition where they could have gotten ailments or parasites from different reptiles or creatures of land and water.

CHAPTER SEVEN

FIRST AID DEVICES, MORE EXPLANATION ON DISEASES PLUS DISORDERS YOU SHOULD KNOW REGARDING CRESTED GECKO

-Gecko First Aid Kit

-Syringe(s)

-Eye dropper

-KY Jelly (ointment)

-Q-tips

-Reptile-safe effective disinfectant (.05% chlorhexidine, Betadine, and so on)

-Tweezers

-Gram Scale

-Expendable gloves

-Amplifying glass

-Pedialyte

Maladies and Disorders

Generally speaking, they are an extremely solid creature and don't consistently become sick. Great farming will forestall most issues. Dietary insufficiencies, for example, metabolic bone sickness, might be the most well-known affliction in peaked geckos and can be dodged with a decent eating regimen.

In the event that you don't give sufficient ventilation, they can get helpless to respiratory contaminations. Whenever kept excessively muggy and they can get bacterial diseases of the skin. Each are effectively treated, yet geckos can wind up passing on because of these effectively preventable issues.

Parasites are additionally a worry; the greatest concern is Entamoeba, which was explained much earlier, is a one-celled critter that causes sensational weight reduction, dormancy and passing. Pinworms (nematodes) are generally to a greater degree an aggravation however a hefty burden in a creature will cause issues. Cryptosporidium is seldom analyzed in peaked geckos yet is as yet a chance.

Crested or peaked gecko MBD

Metabolic bone ailment (MBD) alludes to a need (or unevenness) of calcium in the body, prompting calcium being taken from the bones. MBD in peaked geckos by and large appears as deformed bones, particularly in the spine, hips and tail. Feeble jawbones are additionally an indication of MBD, as are swollen appendages.

Giving a decent eating routine is urgent to forestall this devastating infection!

Parasites

Peaked or crested geckos are powerless to numerous parasitic life forms. There are a few parasites that require a mediator have (like a creepy crawly that thusly gets eaten by the reptile) so as to finish the lifecycle. Regardless of whether you eliminate the first optional host, it's conceivable the parasite can relocate to another one.

Different ailments are spread by microorganisms (particularly salmonella as was explained before), viri, and growths. Wild-got creatures are the well on the way to host and give parasites to other people. Indeed, even hostage reared creatures can convey parasites at levels that may not be recognized in a couple of fecal tests, or they probably won't cause unjustifiable difficulty on the creature so they seem sound. Blending creatures even of similar species conveys danger of parasite transmission.

Probably the most destructive and fatal parasites are protozoa: unicellular eukaryotic creatures that incorporate single adaptable cell (like savage entamoeba), coccidia and Cryptosporidium. Supposed "worms" are nematodes that live in the digestive system and now and again really help with assimilation in some herbivorous creatures. As they are frugivorous just as insectivorous, it is conceivable they utilize harmonious creatures to help separate their food;

however there have not been any examinations as far as anyone is concerned. Note that there can be various strains (vertebrate just, reptile-just, and so forth) of each kind and typically found as pathogenic in their focused on gathering of creatures.

Entamoeba invadens (Amoeba) – has been known to destroy peaked gecko assortments moderately rapidly. Signs incorporate quick weight reduction. Can be treated with Flagyl (metronidazole) with incredible achievement.

Pinworm (Nematode) – a typical distress in cresties; episodes for the most part present with obvious worms in the defecation joined by a more terrible than regular smell.

Treated with Panacur (Fenbendazole) with extraordinary achievement.

Cryptosporidium (Sporozoan) – another "squandering sickness" brought about by protozoan parasites. Can be treated with paromomycin yet the gecko will consistently be "crypto-positive". May shed the parasite and contaminate different reptiles. Rare finding in Rhacodactylus, yet conceivable. Cryptosporidiosis isn't treatable.

Impaction

Ingesting unfamiliar material (hair, substrate, and so forth) can bring about a blockage in the gut.

Shedding Problems

Reptile ecdysis, or shedding, is a typical aspect of their development and digestion. At the point when a peaked gecko has an awful shed, they may require your assistance or the skin may contract blood stream, prompting loss of toes, tail tips or even a whole foot (extremely uncommon). These generally happen when the gecko is youthful, as hatchlings and adolescents can dry out rapidly and not have sufficient dampness to shed totally. Check them every now and again at each taking care of to guarantee they don't have stuck shed on their toes or tails. Now and again they will have little shreds adhered to their hooks, which don't cause an issue. Peruse more about adhered shed and what to do about it.

Wound Care

There is no "best" treatment for minor injuries, yet the accompanying skin disinfectants and emollients can be valuable for minor issues. In geckos, little injuries by and large recuperate up fine as-will be the length of it is a minor injury, similar to a tail nip.

Neosporin is incredible at eliminating germs yet the oil in it may diminish skin recuperating. Be that as it may, it keeps the injury sodden. There is a non-oil Neosporin cream that is better, as long as it doesn't have any painkillers, which can be savage to herps.

Silver sulfadiazine cream is extraordinary, yet you may need to get it from a vet.

Nectar could likewise be utilized, however then it's high in sugar and might hold life forms that feed on sugars, or draw in flies to the injury.

An appropriately weakened (0.05%) chlorhexidine arrangement is extraordinary in the event that you have it, simply be certain it is exceptionally weakened as it can possibly hurt the skin at higher fixations. In any case, I utilize the stuff at surface disinfectant fixation and it doesn't appear to aggravate human or reptile skin. I've likewise utilized it at that quality on tail nips and saw no negative response. In any case, you should comply with the headings and go for a .05% weakening.

Egg Binding (Dystocia)

Eggs that are not laid at the fitting time can expand during their turn of events and become stopped in the pelvic support. Causes can be healthful insufficiencies (particularly calcium), powerless muscle tone, and farming issues identified with mugginess and absence of fitting home destinations.

Pre-ovulatory follicular balance is a related issue, wherein the typical creation of eggs is interrupted, bringing about numerous phases of shelled and unshelled eggs creating in the regenerative lot of females. On the off chance that the female can't totally shell and remove the eggs as in ordinary ovulation, they can remain in the body cavity as semi-created eggs if not reabsorbed. Medical procedure may then be important to

eliminate the majorities, which take after a
group of grapes sometimes.

As size is the standard marker of sexual
development, hostage reptiles are regularly
more youthful than their wild partners when
they arrive at reproducing size. As pre-
ovulatory balance has not been found in the
wild, it is conceivable that quick
development in hostage reptiles can prompt
regenerative issues, particularly in creatures
short of what one year old enough.

THE END

Printed in Great Britain
by Amazon

50182574R00040